Your Vote, Your Voice

Elise Wallace

Reader Consultants

Jennifer M. Lopez, M.S.Ed., NBCT
Senior Coordinator—History/Social Studies
Norfolk Public Schools

Tina Ristau, M.A., SLMS
Teacher Librarian
Waterloo Community School District

iCivics Consultants

Emma Humphries, Ph.D.
Chief Education Officer

Taylor Davis, M.T.
Director of Curriculum and Content

Natacha Scott, MAT
Director of Educator Engagement

Publishing Credits

Rachelle Cracchiolo, M.S.Ed., *Publisher*
Emily R. Smith, M.A.Ed., *VP of Content Development*
Véronique Bos, *Creative Director*
Dona Herweck Rice, *Senior Content Manager*
Dani Neiley, *Associate Content Specialist*
Fabiola Sepulveda, *Series Designer*

Image Credits: cover rypson/iStock; p5 Sundry Photography/Shutterstock; p15 Kauka Jarvi/Shutterstock; p16 Steve Helber/Asociated Press; pp18-19 Fotosearch/Stringer/Getty Images; p21 Rob Crandall/Shutterstock; pp24-25 Everett CollectionShutterstock; all other images from iStock and/or Shutterstock

Library of Congress Cataloging-in-Publication Data

Names: Lacey, Saskia, author.
Title: Your vote, your voice / Elise Wallace.
Description: Huntington Beach, CA : Teacher Created Materials, [2021] | Includes index. | Audience: Grades 2-3 | Summary: "Let's get ready to vote! Learn about the issues. Study the candidates. Make your choice and head to the polls!"-- Provided by publisher.
Identifiers: LCCN 2020043712 (print) | LCCN 2020043713 (ebook) | ISBN 9781087605050 (paperback) | ISBN 9781087619972 (ebook)
Subjects: LCSH: Voting--United States--Juvenile literature. | Elections--United States--Juvenile literature.
Classification: LCC JK1978 .L33 2021 (print) | LCC JK1978 (ebook) | DDC 324.60973--dc23
LC record available at https://lccn.loc.gov/2020043712
LC ebook record available at https://lccn.loc.gov/2020043713

5482 Argosy Avenue
Huntington Beach, CA 92649-1039
www.tcmpub.com

ISBN 978-1-0876-0505-0
© 2022 Teacher Created Materials, Inc.

The name "iCivics" and the iCivics logo are registered trademarks of iCivics, Inc.

Table of Contents

Your Vote Is Your Voice

In the United States, adult citizens can **vote**. They choose their leaders. They vote for the president.

Before voting, there is a lot to think about. The country faces many **issues**. Which ones are important? What each person thinks matters. A person's vote is their **voice**!

This boy thinks things through. Maybe he is thinking about important issues.

It's Easy....
VOTE
....It MATTERS!

HT FOR
OMEN
HT 4
OMEN

Jump into Fiction

First-Time Voter

There is an election soon. Elle is excited. Her sister Hope has just turned 18. Hope will be voting for the first time!

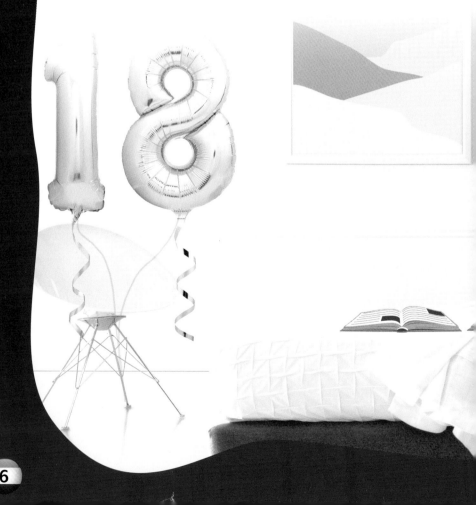

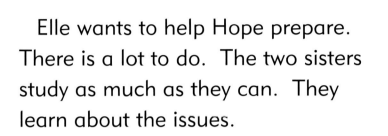

Elle wants to help Hope prepare. There is a lot to do. The two sisters study as much as they can. They learn about the issues.

There are some issues Hope cares about. She cares about schools. She cares about having nice roads. Hope also thinks health care should cost less.

Elle and Hope learn about the people running for office. The sisters want to find someone who shares Hope's views. They do a lot of research. Soon, Hope is ready. She can't wait to vote!

Back to Nonfiction

One issue some people care about is recycling.

Finding Your Voice

You are **unique**. Your view of the world is unique. That is a good thing! Each person has their own experiences. Each person has different views of how the world should be. One idea does not always work for everyone.

Find out what is important to you. What issues do you care about? Think about these issues. Talk with people you trust. Talk with people who have different ideas. Decide what you think should be done. This will help you find your voice.

Issue: Education

Some people think schools need more money. This money may be used to buy new books. It may be used to repair old buildings. It may be used to hire more teachers.

Someday, you may get to vote for president. As you prepare to vote, study the world around you. Look at things such as schools and parks. Can they be improved or made better? Think about how you would change where you live. What does your community need the most?

Issue: Government

Some people think government should be in charge of more services. Other people think government should not be in charge of so much.

✦ Think and Talk

How can leaders and the public work together to make things better?

Leaders think about issues. They think about parks and schools. They think about health care and jobs. They study these issues. Voters should study the issues too!

Issues are big ideas. They take a lot of care and thought. As you study, you will form opinions. Those beliefs will help you find your voice. This is how you prepare to vote.

You can study issues on the internet.

Some workers earn minimum wage.

Issue: Jobs

Some people think the **minimum wage** should be higher. Some people think it should stay the same.

Three candidates speak at a debate.

The Candidates

Learn about people who are running for president. They are called candidates. They want to lead the country.

One way to learn is to watch the **debates**. Candidates talk about their views in the debates. You can learn a lot.

Read about candidates too. Ask questions. What does each person say they will do? Do they have the power to keep those promises? Do you agree with their plans?

Think and Talk

How does this photo support what is said in the text?

Compare each candidate. Study them carefully. How are their views alike? How are they different? Whom do you agree with?

The person you vote for should match your views. They should care about the issues you care about.

Who Can It Be?

A person must be at least 35 years old to be president. They must also have been born in the United States.

Abraham Lincoln was a candidate in the first debate for president.

At the Polls

Now it is **election** time. Voters know the issues. They are ready to choose! They know the person they want to be president.

People go to the **polls**. Each voter is assigned a polling place. They cast their votes with other Americans. Some people have to stand in line for hours. They know it is important to vote!

Poll workers check in voters.

Don't Forget!

You must be 18 years old to vote for president. You must also **register** to vote. You might fill out a form and mail it in. In some states, you can register online.

Not everyone goes to the polls to vote. Some people mail in a **ballot** ahead of time. Some people can do this if they know they cannot make it to the polls.

It doesn't matter *how* a person votes. It just matters that they do!

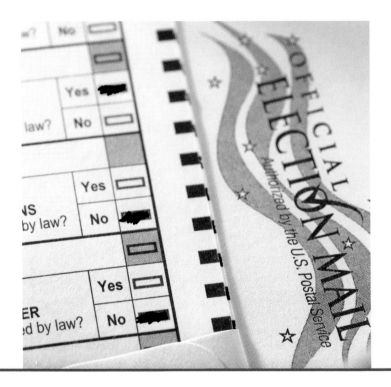

Absent Voters

When people vote by mail, they use an *absentee ballot*. It means that people can mail in their ballots or drop them off.

This woman votes.

The Results

After voting, the wait begins. Who will win the election? Around the country, people watch and wait. Some will celebrate. Others may not.

The person you voted for may not win. Don't give up. Keep voting! Your vote tells the leaders who do win about your hopes, dreams, and needs.

Your chance to vote may seem far away, but it really isn't. Take time now to find the issues you care about. Help your family and friends prepare for voting too!

Glossary

ballot—a sheet of paper or a ticket that is used to vote in an election

debates—events where people share their opinions on topics

election—an event where people vote

issues—subjects that people are thinking and talking about

minimum wage—the least amount of money per hour that workers can be paid

polls—the places where people vote during elections

register—put your name on an official list

unique—very special and unlike others

voice—a person's wish, opinion, or feeling

vote—to make an official choice for a person or an idea

Index

Civics in Action

One thing citizens do is vote. We can vote about issues such as health care and schools. It is good to practice this responsibility. It is important to study the issues. This helps us make good choices when we vote.

1. Talk with your class about a few important issues. They can be things in your neighborhood, city, state, or country.

2. Learn more about one of these issues. Decide what you think about it.

3. Discuss the issues with others.

4. Hold a class vote on all these issues.

5. Discuss the results.